Editor Michael Andre
Associates Elena Bakaitis, Suzanne Ostro,
Robert Buecker, John Coletti, Stacy
Miller, Rosie Schaap, Robert Bower,
Grace Wing-Yuan, Jonas Mekas

Arcifanfaro, King of Fools is an issue of *Unmuzzled OX*. Printed
in U.S.A. ISBN 0-934450-57-9. This is *Unmuzzled OX* volume
XV nos. I-4, US-ISSN 0049-5557. Copyright 2001, Michael
Andre and The Estate of W.H.Auden. Subscriptions are $20 a
year. We have a Yahoo! message board and gallery; email
us for an invitation: MAndreOX@AOL.com. All orders,
subscriptions and correspondence should be sent to Ourtario
Literature P.O.Box 550 Kingston K7L 4W5 Ontario Canada or
Unmuzzled OX 105 Hudson Street New York 10013

May Wilson Twice by Rusty Russell, 1968

Unmuzzled OX was a magazine of the late twentieth century. Then the twentieth century got later and later and and finally went off-line. Ho-boy -- clip art! I finally used some. Yes, we have a new computer. But the text looks better on the monitor than it ever could black-and-white on this page. So the new computer, like this new century, is so far a big disappointment.

Many contributors and friends of **OX** resided wholly in that last century -- **May Wilson**, Rudy Burckhardt, John Cage, Allen Ginsberg, James Dickey, Robert Duncan, Douglas Woolf, John Unterecker, Hannah Weiner, Hannah

Green, Isabella Gardner, Hannah Wilke, Diane Arbus, Helen Adam, James Wright, Hannah Weiner, Andy Warhol, Romare Bearden, Charles Bukowski, Joe Brainard, Ray Johnson, James Lee Byars, W. S. Burroughs, Dick Higgins, Virgil Thomson, Ezra Pound, Kathy Acker, Denise Levertov, David Ignatow, General Idea and Wystan Hugh Auden.

Auden was born in York, England, in 1907. Carlo Goldoni was born in Venice in 1707. Opera was invented in Venice around 1605. What was that like? A first performance of *Merchant of Venice* was noted in 1605: Sordidone in our play is very like Shylock.

But Goldoni wrote *Archifanfano* in 1749, the year Goethe was born.

I knew Auden only in that I spent an hour with him asking questions and drinking tea. (This interview is in **Unmuzzled OX, volume I, number 3, 1972.** You're holding, by that numerology, **volume XV 1-4, 2000.** Our "volumes" are not annual. Bibliographically we're called "an occasional of the arts.")

In preparing for the interview, I read everything Auden wrote, and then tried to cozen Lincoln Center out of a tape of *Rake's Progress*; recordings were then unavailable; but I needed Auden or Stravinsky's written permission, and I finally figured I was lucky to get Auden's acquiescence to the interview -- which appeared with a cover portrait of Auden by **Laurie Anderson.** At the time, Laurie was my girlfriend's roommate. We were grad students at Columbia. Auden was often around Columbia too at the time, and I could repeat the impressions.

Carlo Goldoni wrote his memoirs.

He didn't confess to rakish behavior. He does mention Casanova's mother but she was evidently more discreet than Casanova *fils* -- or even, say, Jean-Jacques Rousseau. In 1761, Goldoni settled in Paris. The inventor of modern Italian theatre wrote his memoirs, like Casanova, in French. Voltaire touted him as the Italian Molière; Goldoni's still more popular in France than Britain or America. But in the French Revolution, Goldoni's pension as a royal tutor was cancelled, and he died old, poor, and briefly forgotten.

Laurie was writing for *ArtNEWS*, and soon I was too. In 1976 I wrote an article for *Village Voice* on Buecker & Harpsichords, a non-profit art gallery or "alternative space." When Buecker re-organized in 1979 to concentrate on music for the harpsichord, I was invited on the board. The new organization was called The SoHo Baroque Opera Company. In 1983, the shelter of *Unmuzzled OX* collapsed, and since then, the opera company has been our publisher.

Introduction

For the opera company, I started translating operas. The singers would know, that way, what they were singing. The company, you see, chooses its operas based on the music. To me, a poet and literary editor, this seemed strange and absurd. But the tune's the thing in opera.

After interviewing Auden, I finally saw *Rake's Progress*. And then, working with 18th century French texts for the opera company, I started to think about Rimbaud in *"Voyelles."* An issue of *Unmuzzled OX* was announced, entitled *Poems to the Tune*.

Martha Wilson of Guerrilla Girls contributed a shock-jock "parody" -- new words with a satirical twist to a familiar pop song. In terms of musical language, Charles Morrow, Robert Creeley and Kenward Elmslie dealt with more nuanced and, in Elmslie's case, hilarious matters.

Then Robert Wilson, author of *Modern Book Collecting* (and May Wilson's nephew), sent me portions of Auden's unpublished translation of the libretto of an 18th century opera, *Arcifanfano*.

I glanced quickly through it, and saw some of the best Auden poetry I'd ever read, whether original or "translation."

This was exciting.

Furthermore, Karl Ditters von Dittersdorf, the composer, was one of our SoHo Baroque heroes.

Poems to the Tune

Karl Ditters also wrote his memoirs. He died a little later but not less miserably than Goldoni. The French, when they have their Revolutions, ruin the world. He had been a virtuoso violinist. He had audiences with Frederick the Great and Maria Theresa.

But he was also a good shot. Out hunting in Silesia he so impressed the local lord that he was made a forester, and soon a minor noble. Karl Ditters became Karl Ditters von Dittersdorf.

Dittersdorf was based in Vienna, and formed a triumvirate there with Gluck and Haydn. They were the tribunal of taste. Dittersdorf's remarks on music, his remarks on Mozart for example, are judicious.

However the Enlightenment featured the apparently wasteful practise of many composers competing to write the best music to the same libretto. Dittersdorf was the fifth composer to write music for Carlo Goldoni's libretto *Arcifanfano*.

Only extraordinary libretti are set by five composers.

6

77 St Mark's Place
New York City
N.Y. 10003

Feb 5th, 1972

Dear Mr André,

Thank you for your letter. I have
no objection to an interview if we
can find a date convenient to us
both. My telephone number is GR 3-0331.
Hope you are over your flu.

your sincerely
W.H. Auden

But then this *Arcifanfano* was lost in the Estrahazy Archives until after World War II. Newell Jenkins then found it there, as well as an additional aria sewn into the text by Haydn.

And then Jenkins commissioned in 1963 this translation from Kallman and Auden. It was mounted at Carnegie Hall by the Clarion Society in 1965 and recorded live.

The recording is now available from VAI Audio, 158 Linwood Plaza (#301), Fort Lee NJ 07024.

It's well regarded: I've heard it on WQXR-FM, the Metropolitan Opera's home station, twice.

Arcifanfaro

Arcifanfano or *Arcifanfaro?* Auden writes Arcifanfaro, Goldoni in his *Mémoires* says -- *Rome est une pepiniere de Chanteurs: nous en trouva^mes deux bons, et six de passables: nous donna^mes, pour premier Intermede, Arcifanfano Re de' Pazzi (le Rois des Fous) musique de Buranello*-- yes it goes on and on, in the best fucking language on earth. Unfortunately this hideous American-made computer is not up to French. Readers of the last **OX**: *Guide des Poètes au Canada* know my loathing, as a Quebecois, for English. I anticipate a third referendum in Quebec, a unilateral declaration of independence, the suspension of the Quebec legislature, civil war, and a million casualties, all French-speaking. Quebec will be re-named Ourtario. But the dead will be martyrs to the best fucking language on earth, French.

Our genius, Goldoni, gave up Italian for French. He understood language *gloire*. Although French is the best language, Italian, with its open vowels, is usually considered the best language for opera. Auden and Kallman translated the Italian of Arcifanfano into English. Auden translated from German and Italian but not French; French can neither be improved nor translated. This should never be forgotten. As the corpses heap up in Quebec, remember -- French is better than Greek and Latin.

Greek and Latin are dead languages, because the Greeks and the Latins didn't have the guts to die for them.

Getting back to opera--

In Praise of Folly

In 1929, John Black translated Carlo Goldoni`s *Mémoires*. This is how he rendered the sole passage on our opera: "It was agreed that the Neapolitans should give their usual sketches, diversified with musical interludes, the subjects of which I should arrange from parodied airs; and this project was in a few days carried into execution.

"Rome is a nursery of singers. We procured two good, and six tolerable ones. The first interlude we gave was "Arcifanfano, Re di Pazzi," the music by Buranello. This little spectacle afforded great pleasure, and the theatre of Tordinona succeeded in a way that prevented the count from being a great loser."

Jenkins' production of Arcifanfaro starred Eleanor Steber as Gloriosa and Anna Russell as Garbata.

Burano, Venetian Isle

My research into this opera was complicated by the Italian habit of naming someone after their birthplace. Baldassare Galluppi, for instance, is known as Il Buranello because he comes from Burano. The libretto to *Archifanfano* was published in Italian but the author was listed, following

9

eighteenth century practise, as Baldassare Galuppi. Goldoni is nowhere mentioned in the text.

The Baroque is a European phenomenon which began with the Counter-Reformation and ended, or was that the Enlightenment? or Everything in General? with the French Revolution. The Baroque was enlightening. Perhaps the Baroque ended with the Rococo. The Romantic Era, on the other hand, was altogether *sturm und drang*, and more rational than common sense would normally or sanely permit. But Byron was greater than Voltaire. Byron, after Shakespeare, was the greatest English poet. And Shakespeare was really, like Auden and Goldoni, a man of the theatre.

Auden liked *The Magic Flute* enough to do a separate edition of his translation.

Hogarth, maker of the original Rake's Progress, was baroque; but Baba the Turk, from the Auden/Stravinsky opera, was borrowed from Byron's Don Juan. Robert Creeley remarked to me, after attending the premiere of yet another terrible Virgil Thomson opera, that Thomson should have chosen Kenneth Koch as his librettist. It's true -- if you can turn out Ottava Rima, and Kenneth like Auden and Byron is a master, then opera libretto should be a snap.

What's Opera, Doc? was recently voted (in a survey of top animators conducted by Jerry Buck) number one among the top fifty cartoons of all time. Whoa! Is that heavy? Or what?

Chuck Jones had Bugs and Elmer Fudd do the complete Ring Cycle in six minutes.

Similarly, when I ordered opera cartoons from the Cartoon Bank, that *New Yorker* subsidiary, they all seemed to make fun of Wagner, especially the Ring, though Tristan's good for a few yucks (cf. "The Wasteland."). Wagner made what you could call Grand Opera. With Mozart, we have the first classic operas that are in the repertory of every two-horse Met, a tradition whose peak is Verdi, which ends with Puccini, and which is (I suppose) master of theatrical laughter and parody in itself.

What's Opera, Doc? Poetry Buffa?

I have edited the typescript using the principles Edward Mendelson uses in Auden's *Libretti*. I have not pared down the repetitious refrains of an opera libretto. But, as Mendelson notes, Auden loved opera not for its music but because it was "the last refuge of the grand style." He liked it for the reason that Yeats liked the Noh.

Think of this play as a verse collaboration between Auden and Goldoni.

Chester Kallman? Kallman taught Auden about opera, he was Auden's first reader, he probably spoke better Italian, and he wrote several interesting poems; however, the only person who ever called Kallman an important writer was his lover, W.H.Auden.

English spelling in the typescript, which we occasionally correct to the logical Canadian spelling, shows Auden's dominance of the American, Kallman.

The play is typical of Goldoni's classic prose plays in that the female characters are stronger and more curious than the male.

It begins in an 18th century immigration office. The identity of the state is concealed until the last scene of the last act. The characters are typical of Goldoni's theatre, and those characters are thoroughly rounded. I never get the sense in Goldoni's theatre, as I do in, say, Dryden's, that the characters are other than life-like.

11

Ostensibly however the characters in this play are madmen. Semplicina is obviously the late Diana Spencer, Princess of Wales. But the madness here, while not benign, is more a matter of folly -- or even the imagination. It is in the Christian tradition of Erasmus, whose *Moriae Encomium (In Praise of Folly)* has influenced everyone from Shakespeare through Milton, Goldoni, and Voltaire to Auden. Opera frequently involves madness; see the CD *Opera Goes Nuts* (EMI/Angel; 1991). What is madness? Is Garbata sane?

Poetry has a hard time without metaphysics. Erasmus threw at Luther's determinism freedom of the will and the poetry of folly. The one Goldoni play transformed posthumously into opera used one of his prose plays *I Quatro Rusteghi*. Prose! I hate it.

Wystan, the Songster

Anna Russell as Garbata (in Newell Jenkins' premiere of the Auden/Dittersdorf version) revived for brilliant moments the *commedia dell arte alla improviso* (which Goldoni transcended) by throwing in McCartney-Lennon riffs. Garbata does not mean in Italian 'Garbage' but 'kindly, gentle.'

She's likeable, wisely foolish.

Auden, in translating the play, translated the name of the titular hero. Faro is a game the Venetians played; fanfares were much loved by Louis. He's more than a king; he's pharoah.

Goldoni despised his warrior brother -- Furibondo is not attractive. The females excite Goldoni's curiosity. They are his only heroes. He hated ferocity. He felt he knew enough about men -- men in Goldoni are uxorious, violent, loud, greedy or foppish. Above all, men make ignominious gambles. Women triumph.

The play's structured as inverted pyramid.
Archifanfaro ends locked inside alive.
Like Yeats and Shakespeare, it's all poetry.

Have yourselves a happy new era. *Vive le Quebec libre!*

OXOXOX!

Arcifanfaro, King of Fools; *or, It's Always Too Late To Learn*
was first presented at Town Hall by the Clarion Music Society.
It was recorded in 1965 and is available from VAI Audio at
109 Wheeler Ave., Pleasantville NY 10570. The cast of this
recording is as follows:

Gloriosa..Eleanor Steber
Garabata..Anna Russell
Semplicina...Patricia Brooks
Sordidone...John McCollum
Furibondo..Heinz Rehfuss
Arcifanfaro...David Smith
Malgoverno..Joseph Sopher

Conductor: Newell Jenkins

Dittersdorf's original version, called *Arcifanfano, re de' matti*,
was first performed at Esterhaza in the autumn of 1777. The
cast was as follows:

Arcifanfano..Catharina Boschwa
Furibondo...Vito Ungricht
Garabata...Maria Anna Tauber
Malgoverno...Pietro Gherardi
Semplicina..Maria Anna Buttler
Sordidone..Leopold Dichtler

ARCHIFANFARO

or

IT'S ALWAYS TOO LATE TO LEARN

Comic Opera in Three Acts

Text by Goldoni,

Music by Dittersdorf

English Version by W. H. Auden &

Chester Kallman

ACT I
Outside the Walls

The King accepts applications for citizenship in his mad capital from Furibondo, who is made keeper of the gate; Gloriosa, who is named siren in residence; Sordidone, who is to become banker to the wasteful; Malgoverno, who is appointed commander to the stupid; Garbata, who is created instructress in folly; and Semplicina.

Chorus
We've travelled far, but here we are, outside this
    fair citee;
'Tis Archifanfaro we seek his subjects for to be:
To Audience
If you desire, we will retire, re-entire presently.

Exit Chorus. Enter Archifanfaro

Archifanfaro
Six new lunatics roam here,

17

Have come from far in hopes of making there home
    here,
Wait now without:
But, in order to discover what kinds of fever are
    coursing through them,
Separately, one by one, we will interview them.
To your task, you who number the increasing
    population
Of lunatics that dwell under our domination,
Get you paper by bales and ink by the barrel
To inscribe their names, their humors, their apparel.

Enter Chorus

Chorus
Long life to Archifanfaro, so great and generous!
For such as we, his rule would be a fate felicitous.
To Audience:
If you allow, we'll come in now, that he may
    welcome us.

Enter Furibondo

Archifanfaro
Approach! What is your name, Sir?

Furibondo
Sir Furibondo I am,
Renowned for valorous deeds from Spain to Siam.

Archifanfaro
Your calling, if I may ask?

Furibondo
It's my profession
To teach all those who cross my path a lesson:
He who rashly dares to flout me,
I bash about and demolish,
Shred him, behead him, abolish.
I am blunt and plain and lacking
In courtly polish.

Archifanfaro
Bravo, Fire-blood-and-thunder!
I, also, when punctured by a tiny mosquito,
Do sunder it and split it,
Hit it, cosh it and squash it --
Royal blood should not ever
Flow incognito.
So, welcome to our city!
And because red blood is in your veins, not water,
Of all our city gateways
Be now the porter.

Furibondo
I'll guard both your bricks and your mortar;
And whomsoever gives me a look orgulous or
          contrary
I will knock down, the gate also, if necessary.

Archifanfaro
But, renowned Furibondo, who makes all warriors
          dither,
What reason, what purpose has brought you
          hither?

Furibondo
Anger drove me from home, fury and high
      dudgeon.
Among men too inferior to know their superior,
I could no longer sojourn:
Their vulgarity, so base, so sycophantic,
Was driving me quite frantic.
So I have come here, hoping you, Archifanfaro,
Your Lordship,
Will honor my valor and swordship:
If not, the hills I'll belabor
With my long and formidable saber.

{aria}
With a sword that is sterner than Moses
I will cut off my enemies' noses,
And all, and all, and all, and all,
All shall beware of my frown.
First, a left swipe!
Then, a right swipe!
There's a leg off!
There's a head off!
In a twinkling
All shall fall down.

Out you varlets!
Come and fight me!
I will send you in hundreds to Hades,
See how luminous, numinous, my blade is,
Luminous, numinous, prominent, dominant, my
      blade is!
Let the haughty, the mighty,
The haughty, the mighty,

The high and the mighty,
Let the high and the mighty
Beware of my frown,
Let the high and the mighty
Beware of my frown:
All, all, shall bow down,

I will cleave their bright helmets asunder,
I am whirlwind and lightning and thunder;
All the kings of the earth shall bow down.
With a lunge here,
And a plunge there,
First I split one,
Then I spit one:
And all, and all fall down.

Come you **varlets**!
Out to battle!
I will shake your thick heads till they rattle!
See how luminous, numinous, my blade is!
Prominent, dominant, my blade is!
Beware of my frown!
Let the high and the mighty
Beware of my frown,
For the haughty, the high and the mighty,
The high and the mighty,
They all, all, all, all, all shall fall!

Exit Furibondo

Archifanfaro
Unhappy oddling, ever wretched and miscreated,
To be laughed at rather than hated:

Young boys admire as a model the
    choleric-ecstatic,
But the old and the rich are mostly phlegmatic.

Enter Gloriosa

Gloriosa
You, they say, are Archifanfaro.

Archifanfaro
It's normal
To curtsey to Kings and speak more formal.

Gloriosa
I will never so to Us be disloyal.

Archifanfaro
Is your lineage royal?

Gloriosa
Can't you see it?

Archifanfaro
I intended no malice.
In what land is your palace?

Gloriosa
In the land of beauty supremely I she it.

Archifanfaro
That is a dominion too subject to plots and
    treasons,
And can endure at most thirty-two seasons.

22

Gloriosa
The thirty-three perfections
That win all men's affections
In me are all united, combined and harmoniously
    mingle,
Of thirty-three I am not lacking a single.

Archifanfaro
Then I must be fairer than you, by Acheron and
    Styx!
My winning points add up to...thirty-six.

Gloriosa
What you say I cannot quite follow,
My beautiful head is hollow;
In figure and in feature,
I'm a miracle, a marvelous creature.

Archifanfaro *Aside*
O blessed happy confusion,
For this madness is immune to all disillusion!
To Gloriosa:
But what reason, dear lady, what cause or purpose
    is it
Brings you on this visit?

Gloriosa
Because this planet is not worthy of me, because
    no one
Perceives I am not a low one,
An ordinary woman, a mere female prepared for
Simply being respected, beloved and cared for.

Archifanfaro
But, surely, this planet is teeming with crazy
     suitors,
For a gentleman made is
To love the fair, woo, admire, pursue the ladies.

Gloriosa
For me, though, such an effect by no means
     suffices,
Because my amazing beauty precious beyond price
     is:
Therefore, I ask you, Arcifanfaro,
Pray you -- may my prayer be granted! --
That I your realm may enamor,
Cause it to stare and stammer,
To gawk and gape at my glamour,
That you may see your subjects by me enchanted.

Archifanfaro
By all means, by all means, Lady,
Do what you can to render
Any wits they have unsteady,
At least, all those who are not mad already.

Gloriosa {aria}
My fair skin,
My bare chin,
How lovely they are!
My true charms,
My two arms,
Shed lustre afar;
The sight of my shoulders

Shall dazzle all beholders,
The world shall adore me
And follow my star.

My gold locks,
My old hocks,
How lovely they are!
My ten toes,
Immense nose,
Shed lustre afar:
The thought of my belly
Shall turn them all to jelly,
The world shall adore me
And follow my star,
My star, my star, my star, my star.
The world shall follow my star.
The sight of my shoulders
Shall dazzle all beholders,
The world shall adore me
And follow my star.

My knee-caps,
My wee paps,
How lovely they are!
My rouged lips,
My huge hips,
Shed lustre afar.
My back, if presented,
Would drive you all demented,
You all would adore me
And follow my star.
My fair skin,
My bare chin,

How lovely they are!
The sight of my shoulders
Shall dazzle all beholders,
The world shall adore me
And follow my star,
My star, my star, my star, my star.
Cry ah! Cry Ah! Cry Ah! Cry Ah!
Adore and follow my star.

Exit Gloriosa

Archifanfaro
Was ever there insanity
Like this lady's?
If any vanity here on earth equal to hers is,
I will give up my kingdom and scribble verses.

Enter Sordidone

Sordidone
Away! Let me go, you robbers! I do not want you
          near me,
To see me or to hear me,
For brigands and bandits are you all, I fear me.

Archifanfaro
Who are you, my good fellow?

Sordidone
My griefs have turned me yellow.
Without peace or rest I go on toiling,
Dirty crusts of bread my eating,
And sour wine all my drinking,

Fitful my sleeping,
And tattered, ragged, torn and patched my
    clothing.

Archifanfaro
That's obvious! but why?

Sordidone
That I may save my pennies and know my purse is
    swelling,
Because gold is a blessing beyond all telling.

Archifanfaro
So! Then perhaps you are wealthy?

Sordidone
Come into the corner. But be quiet, wary, stealthy.
Look into this! Every day the sum increases.
Here are four thousand ducats in pure gold pieces.

Archifanfaro
Goodness! But tell me truly...
I am as discreet as Solon...
All this money...by work you earned it duly?...
It was not...er..er..stolen?

Sordidone
Fairly gained. You see, I'm a money lender,
And as soon as I've found a prodigal spender,
On his own note of hand I loan it:
He, silly fellow, will gamble, riot and tipple;
So, in short while, my principle I triple;
By his folly he my hoard enlarges:

As percent, forty per month my usual charge is.

Archifanfaro
Faugh, Sordidone! Excuse me!
I like all madmen, but scoundrels...do not amuse.

Sordidone
Unjustly all men abuse me
And would, if they could, misuse me,
Mostly because I've scraped and saved up every
        penny.
My diversions have been few, their delights many:
Scorned and rejected by all men, I have one
        consolation,
Accumulation.

Archifanfaro
Justly they treat you so!
But I am good-natured. Let me say this as a
        warning.
You ought to know
That the crazy have no liking for gold, in fact they
        hate it,
And, whenever they get some, dissipate it.

Sordidone
But that is why I have come here, to your realm as
        a stranger,
For in my own land I am ever in danger.
My neighbors know I have a purse with something
        in it,
So out of doors and in doors, I am pestered and
badgered every minute.

"Glad you are going my way, sir!"
"Isn't it a very fine day, sir!"
A glass of wine, an arm or a carriage they offer,
Every one of them planning to steal my coffer.
Here where, since all men are mad, money's no
      matter,
I ought to get fatter
And, safe from envious ravings,
Be left in peace to enjoy my well-earned savings.

Archifanfaro
Give it to me. I will hold it.
It will be safer with me,
And, if I have not sold it,
In my fist it will be
When I unfold it.

Sordidone
But my Lord....

Archifanfaro
Do you doubt me?
Here doubters are unwelcome, let me tell you.
One little more complaint and I will expel you.

Sordidone
O sir, is it quite safe, sir?

Archifanfaro
I swear it is!
Madmen who keep their word are nature's rarities.

Sordidone

What have I done? Don't leave me! Come back!
Come back!

Archifanfaro
What's the matter?

Sordidone
How can you so upset me?
Farewell, my precious! Never, never forget me!

Archifanfaro
Forgetting your former sadness,
Enter our gates with gladness,
Where I now appoint you, because my choice in
      lunatics is tasteful,
As banker to the careless and all the wasteful.

Sordidone
I will go. I depart.
But please show kindness to my poor little heart.

Archifanfaro
I haven't got it. Is it not safe where Nature placed
      it?

Sordidone
No, in that little box I have encased it.

{aria}
Snugly hidden, safe from prying, safe from prying,
In a box my heart is lying,
Safe, safe,
There my heart is lying,

30

Though my limbs begin to shiver, to shake and
    shiver,
Though disconsolate my liver,
Though I ache in every part,
Though I ache in every part,
Ache in this part, ache in that part,
Ache and smart.
Plagued by snivels and by sneezing,
From my lungs the breath comes wheezing,
And my bowels start to chide me -- How they
    chide me! --
Grumble, rumble loud inside me,
For they miss their little heart.
Ow, my bowels! How they chide me,
Grumble, rumble loud inside me,
For they miss their little heart,
How my bowels ache inside me,
Grumble, rumble loud inside me,
Grumble, rumble and mumble,
Because they miss their heart;
All miss their little heart,
All miss their little heart.

In a box my heart is lying.
Though my limbs begin to shiver,
Though disconsolate my liver,
Though I ache in every part,
Plagued by snivels and by sneezing,
From my lungs the breath comes wheezing,
And my bowels start to chide me.
Grumble, rumble loud inside me,
For they miss their little heart,

Ow, my bowels! Ow, my bowels! How they chide
    me! How they chide me!
Grumble, rumble loud inside me,
For they miss their little heart,

Grumble, rumble and mumble because they miss
    their heart.
My ankles ache, both my elbows ache, my ten
    fingers ache,
Because they miss their heart.
My colon hurts, both my kidneys hurt, my
    gall-bladder hurts,
Because they miss their heart:
All miss their little heart,
All miss their little heart.

Exit Sordidone

Archifanfaro
Madness beyond all measure,
For the sake of treasure,
To go without all pleasure!
The miser is a wretched devil
Who does no good to his neighbor and to himself
    evil.
I, too, can talk like crazy
To buttercup or daisy,
Can mop and mow, too,
But I can say No, too:
Those in royal stations
Ought to keep *some* lucid moments
For state occasions.

Enter Malgoverno

Malgoverno
Archifanfaro!
Unlucky Malgoverno my name is,
To have consumed my fortune, beggared myself
      my shame is,
Taking no thought of the morrow
Till overtaken by sorrow;
Worn by changes, painful, insidious,
I who yesterday was handsome have become
      hideous.

Archifanfaro
That's obvious! But no matter.
For, surely, you still have friends who still remind
      you
Of all the merry times which lie behind you.

Malgoverno
Their welcome soon diminished
When they saw that my money was finished;
Also the women who'd embraced me, called me
Sweeting and Minion,
When there was no more left changed their
      opinion.

Archifanfaro
Your just home have you found, for,
This is where you were bound for.

Malgoverno
Why is it just, Sir?

Archifanfaro
If you could ever trust, Sir,
Women's hearts that cruel are, and fickle, and
        scheming,
You are mad, Sir, and beyond hope of redeeming.

Malgoverno
Bitter the waking that follows sugared dreaming!
Women and men both are greedy,
And to the needy
Are not affectionate, alert and delightful,
But disdainful and spiteful.
Misfortune they shun as a curse,
And when they see it
Run away and flee it.
Desperate I seek your city,
Since it is madness or worse to show pity
When Fate seems to be averse.

Archifanfaro
I will save you and console you
And as a citizen I now enroll you.
Here is a purse
To pay with, to make hay with, to play with,
And I appoint you Commander of the Stupid,
Of their riot and revels the Master-Cupid.

Malgoverno
Long live your Noble Majesty!
I thank you. I'll spend it
All in games and pleasure:
Though my state is no longer splendid

I'll pipe and sing and tread a merry measure.

{aria}
When the purse is clinking, clinking,
    Then the greatest joy we know,
    The greatest joy we know
Lies in drinking and in thinking
    How to make the money go.

If the spoon is golden, golden.
    You were born with, lucky you!
All the more are you beholden
    Your good fortune to get through.
If the spoon is golden, golden,
If the spoon is golden, golden,
    You were born with, lucky you!
All the more are you beholden
Your good fortune to get through.

Exit Malgoverno

Archifanfaro
There, like a vapor or a bubble
Goes the gold the miser gathered with infinite
    trouble.
But who is the modest maiden,
Though not with brains over-overladen?
With someone so fleat and fair
I'd not be loathe to share both my throne and
    kingdom.

Enter Semplicina

Semplicina
Stop it! Stop it! Unhand me, rude beasts!
Keep far away, you lewd beasts!

Archifanfaro
What can have driven such a fair country maid
     from pasture and tillage?

Semplicina
I had to flee my village:
I could not bear to be touched and clutched at,
As would now these madmen,
The horrible bad men!

Archifanfaro
Don't be afraid and come nearer. What is your
     name?

Semplicina
Dear little Semplicina.

Archifanfaro
A housewife? Or a pure virgin?

Semplicina
Fie! Fie! For shame, Sir!
I a married woman? I! Why?
My soul is clean, Sir,
A man's face I've never seen, Sir.

Archifanfaro
What keeps you so incurious?

Semplicina
I am shy, Sir, a little shy, Sir,
That's why, Sir.

Archifanfaro
Then to each other,
Sister your soul, mine bother!
Because I'm also shy by nature, not haughty.

Semplicina
Oh! The men are all so naughty,
Think delicious what is vicious.

Archifanfaro
Maybe, but if you've never tested....

Semplicina
Men are hairy-chested!

Archifanfaro
If in no man's face you've yet been interested.

Semplicina
A girl who is decent looks always in the gutter.

Archifanfaro
If half-witted. If looks are not permitted,
Are there no gentle words a man may utter?

Semplicina
Are you sure, Sir, that they're pure, Sir?

Archifanfaro

To touch your hand does not defy convention?

Semplicina
Not if it be without unseemly intention.

Archifanfaro
I have become a modest maiden,
A pure and virginal ninny,
Ever since I strayed in
The Land of Whipperginny.

Semplicina
O Sir, I beg you, save me! I am helpless and
        blameless.
The men are rude and shameless,
Pursue me with their glances,
With their immodest words and improper advances.

Archifanfaro
Have you no father, no mother?

Semplicina
Why, Sir? Yes.

Archifanfaro
Then why are you still husbandless?

Semplicina
Because...because I can't, when my father and
        mother
Would have me wedded to one, I to another.

Archifanfaro

38

There is some lucky man you sigh for?

Semplicina
And would die for.

Archifanfaro
Of course, he's a second Adonis.

Semplicina
Maybe so.
His face to me still unknown is.
I don't know.

Archifanfaro
Poets in their books like
To sing of love, but not of such a lady
Who has not wondered what her lover looks like.

Semplicina
As maiden pure to Your Majesty I rush
For my safety...O sir...You make me blush.

Archifanfaro
Come closer! You shall discover
What was meant in the old days by a lover,
In old days what a beau meant.
Look at me just a moment!

Semplicina
Ah woe, Sir, I No, Sir!

Archifanfaro
To look at me is not a naughty thing:

Remember I, after all, am only your king.

Semplicina
No, no, no, never!
Except, however,
I might, just possibly, be bold to,
If I were told to.

Archifanfaro
You are. Suppose I'm a sheep of yours.
Now lift your eyes a little; give me a peep of yours.

Semplicina   {aria}
O look so woeful, woeful,
O features adroit and oval,
O features adroit and oval,
O big blue eyes I fear,
They hurt me somehow here,
They hurt me somehow here.
O no, Sir. Let me go, Sir!
I blush and would depart,
To flee from Cupid's dart,
To flee from Cupid's dart
I blush and would depart,
A-ah, a-ah, a-ah, a-ah!
I blush and would depart.
I never dared to scan
The face of any man,
A maid I am at heart,
A maid I am at heart.
I fear for any man
If ever I began!
A maid I am at heart,

A maid I am at heart,
A modest maid at heart,
An honest maid at heart.
O look, so woeful, woeful,
O features droit and oval,
O big blue eyes I fear,
They hurt me somehow here,
They hurt me somehow here.
O mouth so big and burly,
O hair so crisp and curly,
O no, Sir, let me go, Sir,
I blush and would depart.
A-ah, a-ah, a-ah, a-ah!
I blush and would depart.
Although I dream, it's true,
About what lovers do,
I'm still a maid at heart,
I'm still a maid at heart.
I often dream, like you,
About what lovers do,
Though still a maid at heart,
Though still a maid at heart,
A modest maid at heart,
A modest maid at heart.

Exit Semplicina

Archifanfaro
Such as she seem to be frigid,
With principles too rigid:
They blush and retreat and *say* No
But, when you touch them, erupt like some
volcano.

Enter Garbata

Garbata
Hullo, all! Are there none here?
Has the fun here not yet begun here?
I would never have come here if life is glum here.
I like the din so hearty of a party.

Archifanfaro
Brava! damsel exotic!
We need more idiotic
Clowns and fools and tumblers,
Not moaners and grumblers.

Garbata
Please, do you know who I am?

Archifanfaro
Dear Lady, no.

Garbata
I am...I am...I am...I am...O, now I know!
I'm Garbata the Merry,
I'm not a little mad but very;
Regret I won't descend to,
I have never wept in my life and don't intend to.

Archifanfaro *Aside*
Not that she could if she would.

Garbata
In war-time, in peace-time, in sunshine, in rain,

Be it Sunday or Friday,
Always it's a fun-day and my-day,
A holiday, a high-day,
Kingdoms and houses may totter.
Always I'm gay as an otter;
Unbedded, beloved or wedded is no matter:
When Gabriel blows the trumpet I shall chatter.

Archifanfaro *Aside*
O what a fine addition!
I will grant her admission,
Accept her gladly.
My madmen look sadly:
They need her badly.

Garbata
I fled my city like a hare
Because everyone there
Is becoming soulful,
Romantic, wan and doleful,
Will no longer take love and loving lightly,
Changing their affections nightly.
It's now the fashion
To affect a Grand Passion.
Any pleasure they all frown on and look down on.
If seated beside his Laura,
A real up-to-date adorer
Will not eat like any sinner
But sighs his way through dinner.
If he should touch her knee under the table-cloth
And she declines to please him,
What agonies will seize him,
Despair, discommodation and rage in foison!

43

Be it a Sunday or Friday,

Always it's fun-day and my-day,

A holiday, a high-day,

Kingdoms and houses may totter,

Always I'm gay as an otter;

Unwedded, beloved or wedded is no matter:

When Gabriel blows the Trumpet I shall chatter.

ARCH (aside)

O what a fine addition!

I will grant her admission,

Accept her gladly.

My madmen look sadly:

They need her badly.

GARB

I fled my city like a hare

Because everyone there

Is becoming soulful,

Romantic, wan and doleful,

Will no longer take love and loving lightly,

Changing their affections nightly.

It's now the fashion

To affect a Grand Passion.

Any pleasure they all frown on and look down on.

If seated beside his Laura,

A real up-to-date adorer

Will not eat like any sinner

But sighs his way through dinner.

If he should touch her kneed under the table-cloth

Nothing then will ease him
But to go and to take poison.

Archifanfaro
How can people make such pother over one
      another?
Govern such I decline to:
Those who love themselves as mine do
Are much less bother.

Garbata
I mean to stay light-hearted,
Merry as when I started,
No complications, no sudden palpitations.
Your Majesty I greet.
May the heavens preserve and keep you from cold
      and heat!

Archifanfaro
I thank you, I give you welcome, I name you
      teacher,
To learn us the arts of folly;
Of nonsense be thou our preacher.

Garbata
Hurrah, Sir, for folly!

{aria}
Now sing!
Let's all be jolly,
Let's all be jolly,
And banish melancholy,
And banish melancholy.

AND banish melancholy.
HE WILL
This life is but BALL
she won't
a gay
WE DO,
MAD AND CRAZY all
unending BALL
they don't
'Tis but a choice of folly
How crazy are we all
or won't
And if you WILL
And if you do or don't
I'm a madcap
For crazy
And if you
are we all
You're a madcap,
For madcaps are we all.
Mad & CRAZY ALL,
'Tis but a choice of folly
The World in any weather
For madcaps are we all
IS GIDDY as a feather,
So let us Dance together

This life is but a ball,
A gay unending ball,
And if you will or won't,
And if you do or don't,
'Tis but a choice of folly,
For madcaps are we all,
'Tis but a choice of folly
For madcaps are we all.
So come together, dancers,
In waltzes or The Lancers,
Though you be fat and forty,
Look mischievous and naughty.
He will, she won't, we do, they don't,
She will, he won't, they do, we don't,
'Tis but a choice of folly
For madcaps are we all.
I'm a madcap,
You're a madcap,
Mad and crazy all,
Mad and crazy all.
The world in any weather
Is giddy as a feather,
So let us dance together
Until the heavens fall,
If heavens *can* fall.

So sing now:
Let all be jolly,
Let all be jolly.
Who cares what we are here for?
Who knows the why or wherefore?
This life is but a ball,
A gay unending ball,

And whether you love one
Or whether you love none,
'Tis but a choice of folly
For crazy are we all,
'Tis but a choice of folly
For crazy are we all,
Who cares what we are here for?
Who knows the why or wherefore?
The world in any weather
Is giddy as a feather.
Love all, love none, love one, it's fun
And but a choice of folly,
For crazy are we all.
For crazy are we all,
'Tis but a choice of folly
For crazy are we all.
Shake the rafter
With your laughter
Till the heavens fall,
Until the heavens fall,
Until the heavens fall.

Exit Garbata

Archifanfaro
For all forms of illusion
I cherish a fond affection.
To-day I've taken under my royal protection,
As fit to adorn my collection,
Six new types of confusion,
Distinct in hue and complexion,
And, in requital,
The Great Monarch of Madmen shall be my title,

{aria}
The Fierce One lives only
For slaughter and the sword,
The Vain One lives only
To be by all adored,
The Mean One, scorning pleasure,
Lives only for his treasure,
The Prodigal would end it,
Lives only to spend it,
The Prudish One is not quite
As modest as she seems,
The Gay One lives only
For giddy-pated dreams.
The Fierce One
And the Vain One,
The Mean One,
The Mean One,
The Prodigal,
The Prudish One,
The Gay One,
United by folly.
A toast to every folly!
Fa la la la.

Curtain

ACT II, SCENE I
A Chamber
In the Royal Palace

Malgoverno, to whom the King has handed Sordidone's
coffer of gold to squander on revels, offers it in exchange
for Gloriosa's charms. When she spurns it as too little, he
offers it to Garbata, who goes off with him contentedly.
Sordidone, insisting upon the return of his treasure, threatens
-- and even assaults -- Archifanfaro, who escapes by
promising to return it. Desperate, Sordidone decides to hang
himself and enlists Garbata's help with the rope. She throws
it away and restores his coffer to him after he promises to
celebrate its recovery by dancing and singing, which he
unsuccessfully attempts to do. As Garbata and Sordidone
depart, Furibondo rushes about in pursuit of Semplicina, who
fends him off. She sits down to rest and is discovered by the
King. When he sings to her of his love, she finally admits to
being awake -- and joins him in a love duet.

Gloriosa enters. Malgoverno, holding the coffer,
enters through her door and tries to intercept her

Malgoverno
I beg you to stop a second.

Gloriosa
What manners! I won't be beckoned!

Malgoverno
Please! One moment! Without you, life is hollow.

Gloriosa
Don't you know that in splendor, I outshine Apollo?

Malgoverno
Oh turn one loving beam to light me!

Gloriosa
You dare invite me
To disregard ev'ry restraint beauty best holds!?

Malgoverno
Regard then what this chest holds,
Fair goddess, to you presented.
You may have it for one love-beam. I'll be
        contented.

Gloriosa
This coffer
which you proffer --
How much
Do its contents touch?

Malgoverno
Twenty thousand ducats.

Gloriosa
Measured against all my charms, that's ... a drop
     in buckets.

Malgoverno
It's all that I can do.

Gloriosa
The diamonds of Peru
Would not be too much for me really:
Its rubies too,
If they were added genteelly.

Malgoverno
O how priceless are charms when granted freely!
If that is too much to pray for,
There is still much to say for
Any beauty more or less, there'd be less to pay for.

Garbata *Entering and observing Malgoverno on*
     his knees
What on earth are you doing? Can you explain?

Malgoverno
I'm pleading her grace in vain.

Garbata
Such pleas will make you madder.

Malgoverno *To Gloriosa*
You'll grow madder, being pitiless as an adder.

Gloriosa
She is the maddest: she goes gaily
Giving her beauties away, and *I* dare say, daily.

Malgoverno *To Garbata*
My fortune, for a sign of favor,
I, on condition, gave her;
And she refused it, and wasn't even gracious.

Garbata
She is far beyond reason. No, too rapacious.

Malgoverno
Would you accept such an offer from one that
        woos you?

Garbata
Yes, indeed!
Now with greed
Nor to abuse you;
But gratefully to use you,
Lovingly choose you
Mine for dilly and dally,
And to amuse you
Inbetweentimes with songs and ballet!

Gloriosa
Siren! With such-like views, you
Insult Beauty in your charms,
For those who buy charms.

Malgoverno *To Garbata*
If you'd care to
Love me, and swear to,
Adding your charms to your tunes,
I'll give you the latest of all my fortunes.

Garbata
Dearest, if you so honor this courted sweetheart,
You'll be ruler, I swear,
Of my complete heart.

Gloriosa *Aside*
I've been ousted! Unfair!

Malgoverno
Accept this in tribute: I dare est-
eem you 'mongst the fair, the fairest!
You shall dwell in
Place of Helen!
The fullest Beauty, disdainful,
Shall no more reign or remain full.
Long live Beauty when she
To a pitiful plea
Accords her pity.
That is how Beauty should be,
So runs the ditty:

We praise the sun for beauty,
Grateful that its lavish powers
Spend themselves unspent on flowers,
Or meet a sov'reign duty
Subjecting ice and snow,

They meet a sov'reign duty
Subjecting ice and snow;
But beauty earns no praises
That like the north-wind grazes
On hungry eyes and raises
No hope of aught but woe
On hungry eyes it raises
No hope of aught but woe,
No hope of aught but woe,
No hope of aught but woe.
We love the modest roses
Who must blush for their displaying,
Love the lilac who went Maying,
Recall its tender poses
Although by June it died:
And none could love the flower
That will no perfume dower,
Whose bloom adorns a tower
Of mad and wint'ry pride:
But none could love the flower
That will no perfume dower,
Whose bloom adorns a tower
Of mad and wintr'y pride,
Of mad and wintr'y pride,
Of mad and wintr'y pride.

Gloriosa
Bumpkin, coarse-grained, ill-mannered,
Villain too unrefined to
Value Beauty your common vision is blind to!
To Garbata:
And you, quite undeserving, who have usurped the
    rents and duties

Most proper to my beauties,
See you not how it shames you
That he a beauty names you
With me in eye-sight?

Garbata
Your madness shows in my sight:
A madness that's not uncommon
In many sorts of woman --
The ugly, the fair and the plain types
Think only they are right in being such vain types.

Gloriosa
No matter. Though lovely or ugly,
You were wrong to accept his lavish offer:
Because you've robbed the coffer
If you're too plain for a lover;
And a beauty should possess too much decorum
Than to yield to such base hi-cockolorum.

Garbata
I do not care if you're a Gorgon or sea-born Venus,
I do not judge between us,
But *I* know gold is almighty,
And a Fury who has it seems Aphrodite!
Nor is it here the fashion
For swains to sigh with passion:
Either they win the Fair, or losing, they dash on.
With a gift they accomplish their desires:
The proudly stubborn beauty will not maintain her
        squires,
For the tribute that she scorns, another acquires:

Though I am never
Distant or cold,
I like a love-tale
Practic'ly told,
I like a love-tale
Practic'ly told:
Cheats in achieving
Woo self-deceiving,
I love believing
What I behold;
Not self-deceiving,
I love believing
What I behold.
Gifts that delight me
Most I adore,
Not on value
I set store:
Joy brings my will
To the fore --
Happy I will
Love much more,
Happy I will love
So much the more.
I am not one to
Beggar my lovers,
Avid for tributes
Draining their coffers;
But Cupid's arrow
Cuts to my marrow
Tipped on its narrow
Pointer with gold:
Dan Cupid's Arrow
Cuts to my marrow

Pointed with gold,
I love believing
What I behold:
Cupid's arrow
Moves me with gold.

Exeunt Garbata and Malgoverno arm in arm

Gloriosa
No! They cannot persuade me!
If high Jove to play eloper
Became a bull that caught the fancy of Europa,
And Zeus's love could breed a
White swan for Leda,
Or fall in gold for his Danae --
How could I accept a mere man, I?
I shall tarry:
No mortal care I to marry --

Lovely ladies, you enjoying
Holy gifts, Beauty's elected,
Holiest Beauty's elected,
Pride alone can hold protected
What the Proud on high bestow:
What the gods on high with pride bestow.
Lovely ladies,
High decorum holds protected
Holy gifts:
Proud decorum, lovely ladies, holds protected
What the gods on high with pride bestow.
Man whose heart is bent on toying
Flatters charm to charm's destruction:
Beware! By his light seduction,

By his light seduction
Crushed, your beauty's blossom will go.

Lovely ladies, you enjoying
Holy gifts, Beauty's elected,
Holiest Beauty's elected,
Pride alone can hold protected
What the Proud on high bestow;
What the gods with pride bestow:
Man whose heart is bent on toying
To destruction flatters charm,
Lovely ladies, by employing
Proud decorum, hide from harm
What gods bestow,
What the Proud on high bestow,
Lest beauty go.

*Exit Gloriosa. Enter Sordidone
and Archifanfaro by different doors*

Sordidone
Where's my lover
Sweetheart coffer?

Archifanfaro
The coffer has departed.

Sordidone
I'm stunningly broken-hearted.
I'll kill myself, by thunder!
Oh! The mad can be shrewd when there's money
        to plunder.

Archifanfaro
But realise, Sordidone, I've managed for your
protection
By removing the source of your soul's infection.

Sordidone
Can you heart lack?
Bring my heart back.
Bring all and not part back!

Archifanfaro
Sorry buffoon, you'd gain more
If you sought your false heart less and your truthful
brain more.

Sordidone
If I am not unsundered
From that bright heart you've plundered,
I'll crumble away or burst.
But I shall not die lonesome; I'll kill you first!

*Sordidone begins to prod Archifanfaro with a
sword*

Archifanfaro
Ow! Help! Do not go rabid! Madmen! Quickly!
Assist me!

Retainers enter quickly and hold Sordidone

Though wild, he may not long have missed me!
He'll flare higher
If you don't beat out his fire.

Sordidone
Be tender to entreating!
Adding derision to beating
Is a little bit too much.
It cannot bother you much
That I also have lost my treasure.

Archifanfaro
You are justly paying the price for miserly pleasure.

Sordidone
Why am I a miser? Because I spent with caution
And wisely put aside a portion?
To punish me for that I call excuseless.

Archifanfaro
Money was not intended to be useless.

Sordidone
Alas! I've lost my way...the north-winds freeze
        me...
Imps and freezing demons seize me...
Let go!
Who stands before me? Do I know?
Orlando? Mephisto? I defy the arrant chattel!
We shall do battle.

Archifanfaro
Hold on to him! Hold on to him!

Sordidone
Unhand me!

I shall kill the knave who dares to countermand me!
Remain here! Wouldst thou flee?

Archifanfaro
Have you forgotten? I am the lunatic king!

Sordidone
Your title does not mean a thing.
Return what is mine to me --
My heart and soul's king --
Or my rapier will poke you full of holes, King.

Archifanfaro
My dear demented hoarder,
All would soon be in order
If you would let me go and would not rave:
I'll come back here with the coffer that you crave.

Sordidone
Don't believe it....

Archifanfaro
I promise.

Sordidone
Can't conceive it....

Archifanfaro *Aside*
How to flee from these complications I know not....

Sordidone
Go then...stay here,..be off...don't go...yes,
        go...not....

Archifanfaro
Sordidone, be a bunny,
Let me go and let me be,
Be a bunny,
Let me go and let me be:
I'll come back here with your money,
You can truly trust in me,
You can put your faith in me,
My reliability.
I'll be back in one more minute
With your chest and all that's in it,
All that's in it.
Wait in peace and do not do more,
Clear your dark and stormy humour,
Sordidone, and be sunny,
I'll return with all your money:
Wait in peace here, please be sunny,
Be a bunny, wait your money --
How distract this insane sentry?
Who's that coming? Bar his entry!
More assassins! Bar their entry!
I'll evade this insane sentry,
Sordidone --
Now's my only chance to flee.

*Archifanfaro slips out quickly, followed by his
retainers*

Sordidone
Are you hiding? Would you tease me? What? You
        evade me?
Even the King has now betrayed me.

Yes, the wide world of mankind has joined and
      flayed me.
My treasure has been stolen,
My heart has been slapped and slivered:
What burning in my colon!
I'm skewered! I'm shivered!
What has life on earth to offer?
With no coffer
All is hollow:
Lover,
You are gone: I shall be true and follow.
Yes, yes. This rope will serve me to accomplish my
      travels.
What if the noose-knot unravels?
Now I think it's secure and sure to noosen:
When it slips about and tightens, life will loosen.

Enter Garbata

Garbata
What's this? What's that? What's pending?

Sordidone
I shall pend to make an ending.

Garbata
But I do not see a hangman. Is he dressing?

Sordidone
If my way's too distressing
To your informed acumen,
Perhaps you'd act in his place as my hang-woman.

Garbata
Of course. Give the rope in my hands.

Sordidone
Take it then.

Garbata *Throwing the rope away*
That's ended.
That would have been the maddest of all things
     madmen did.
Tell me, what was the reason you wished to take
     your life?

Sordidone
The theft of my coffer. Oh, how deeply I've
     suffered!

Garbata
Silly! Suppose I told you it's been recovered?

Sordidone
Bring it back if it's true!

Garbata
You'll have it back on condition that you...
Will celebrate with me in tootling and trilling,
Shout with joy that's overspilling,
Never again will consider dreary self-killing.

Sordidone
If you arrange that my gold can again on me shine,
Then all the life on earth, with my life, will re-shine!

Garbata
I'll be back before you realise.

Exit Garbata

Sordidone
Oh my darling! Oh my lovely! Where all that's Me
lies.

Garbata *Re-entering with the coffer and giving it to
him*
Here it is. As I promised. So you ought to be
delighted.

Sordidone
I'm emphatic
-Ly ecstatic,
I am united.

Garbata
Now it is time to fulfill what we have plighted.

Exit Garbata

Sordidone *Carefully examining the coffer and after
a bit looking inside*
Poor little baby, they've caressed you:
I hope they haven't undressed you.

Garbata *Re-entering with two guitars, one of which
she gives to Sordidone*
Sounding,

Bounding,
And astounding,
Let us
Quickly get us!

Sordidone
What shall I do, though?

Garbata
With me, come to heel-and-toe,
To singing most featly step it:
We'll rejoice ere our talents become decrepit.
    See comely Phyllis wander
    With Corydon her beau,
Discoursing love they go:
Their time is theirs to squander
    In hither, yonder
And carefree to and fro;
    And fonder and fonder
    They ever grow,
Discoursing as they go.

Sordidone
How carefree I shall wonder
Above, about, below,
With all I worship so:
And never, hither, yonder,
    My treasure squander,
My Corydon bestow;
    And fonder and fonder
    Will Phyllis grow:
I love my shepherd so!

Garbata . . . .
See comely Phyllis wander
With Corydon her beau.
Their time is theirs to squander
In carefree to-and-fro:
Meandering they go
     And fonder, fonder
     Fonder grow.

Sordidone
How carefree I shall wander
Above, about, below,
With all I worship so,
     And fonder grow:
Meandering I go
     And fonder, fonder,
     Fonder grow . . . .

Garbata
Your gold bestows no kisses,
So put it by for me.

Sordidone
Endearing as this,
No object can be.

Garbata
Look well and behold where
A love might be gained.

Sordidone
My love is of gold where
My heart is contained.

Garbata...

See comely Phyllis wander
With Corydon her beau
In carefree to-and-fro:
Their time is theirs to squander,
They love each other so.

Sordidone

How carefree I shall wander
Above, about, below:
I shall never bestow
And never, never squander
This love I treasure so..

Garbata

That you refuse to love me does not jar me:
Enough it is to hear a merry tune struck
That overcomes all sorry sighs of 'Ah! me'
And I sing fondly: Long live in joy the moon-struck!

Sordidone

A joy I must not pay for, works to calm me;
But it's only money that works my heart-strings
        balmy.

Garbata & Sordidone

Upon the mad in whatsoever manner,
The many mad in whatsoever manner,
She smiles in silver moonlight, our goddess Diana,
Our goddess Diana, our moonlight goddess,
Upon our madness in silver moonlight
Diana, our goddess, is smiling,

Diana on madness of manner
Is smiling in moonlight: our goddess Diana.

Exeunt. Enter Semplicina pursued by Furibondo

Semplicina
Don't come near me! Don't come near me!

Furibondo
Do not fear me:
I've no intention to hurt you;
As a matter of fact, I honor your virtue.

Semplicina
I've no need of that honor.

Furibondo
Are you deriding my biding strength?
Rejecting my protection?
Have you weighed that rejection?
When I am angry, men and beasts cry stunned:
        "Oh
Don't reject our entreaties, Furibondo!"

Semplicina
Your name and your attentions
Make me tremble with varied apprehensions.

Furibondo
Kneel down and beg my pardon.

Semplicina
Back, peasant, to your garden.

Furibondo
Peasant? You say that to me!?
Hibbledy-hobbledee!
I'm amazed at my patience: I should, with
    replying,
Have used my might fist to send you high flying,
Should have torn you so apart that now you would
    rubble be.
What on earth can my trouble be?
Well, as Dante says in *Hamlet:*
"It's not the lion's way to harm the lamblet."

The high and the mighty lion
To whom I surely am kin,
When he may chance to spy on
A mild and milk-white lambkin,
A humble milk-white lambkin
That roams his royal path,
His high and mighty path,
His own exclusive path --
The fiercely noble lion
To whom you know I surly am kin,
On spying lambkin
Upon his noble path,
His most almighty path,
His own high noble path,

Is far too grand a creature
To notice her transgression,
Her unaware transgression,
Too generous a creature
To leap and rend her flesh in

His righteous roaring wrath,
His roaring righteous wrath,
His high and mighty wrath.
The king to whom I am kin
Although he spy a lambkin
Has far too grand a nature
To harm the humble creature
Intruding on his path:
Although she's on his path,
He'll not give way to wrath.

Exit Furibondo

Semplicina
Quiet at last. No thump and thunder.
But at least he's less inclined to buss than blunder.
Oh here comes Archifanfaro!
I would like...and I would not like...I must go...
But I must not go...I know now...I don't know...
My heart tells me *yes*...and says *no*...
To observe what's sincere and what's seeming,
I'll pretend to be dreaming....

Enter Archifanfaro

Archifanfaro
What good does a kingdom do me
If my love-life is gloomy?
For I have not held to me
Softly, swoony,
That lady loony.
But there she is! And dreaming!
Gleaming

Are her charms and simple!
How lovely that dimple!
Those lips should sigh *Your Highness....*
What a pity that she's afflicted with shyness.
The problem is most provoking.
But a king must command, or he is no king.
With my royal flare and flash full,
I shall order her regally not to be bashful.
I'll have to wake her. Suppose, though, she runs
          away
When she's awake and knowing?
Maybe I'd best let her sleep to prevent her going.
But if I do not wake her
There is no way to make her
Consider me.
Wakefulness must overtake her:
How shall it be?
I shall arouse her gently as lovingly
I will her name endear her,
Calling softly not too far not too near her...

Semplicina, do you hear me?
Wake, o lovely one, wake to love.

Semplicina *Aside*
Archifanfaro, are you near me?
Come consolingly, wake my love.

Archifanfaro
Dare I wake her? Does she fear me?
In her sleep does she dream of my love?
Semplicina!

Semplicina *Aside*
Archifanfaro!

Archifanfaro
Do you hear me? Do you fear me?
Semplicina!

Semplicina
Archifanfaro!

Archifanfaro
Cupid, steer me.

Semplicina *Aside*
Come, endear me.

Archifanfaro
Wake adoringly.

Semplicina
Come consolingly,

Come consolingly:
Love me, Oh!

Archifanfaro
Wake adoringly:
Love me, Oh!

Semplicina & Archifanfaro
Will the answer be
Yes or no?

Semplicina
Come consolingly...

Archifanfaro
Wake adoringly...

Semplicina & Archifanfaro
Love me, oh!
Will the answer be
yes or no?

Archifanfaro
Semplicina....

Semplicina
Archifanfaro....

Archifanfaro
She must waken!
I am shaken
With amorous dread.

Semplicina
Archifanfaro!

Archifanfaro
Semplicina!

Semplicina *Aside*
Come, command me....

77

Archifanfaro
Fears unmanner me.

Semplicina
With your clemency...

Archifanfaro
With more majesty...

Semplicina
With your clemency
I'd be led.

Archifanfaro
With more majesty
She'd be led

Semplicina
Come consolingly...

Archifanfaro
Wake adoringly...

Semplicina & Archifanfaro
Love me, oh!
Will the answer be
Yes or no?
Will the answer be
Yes or no?

Archifanfaro

78

Semplicina, dream no longer!
Prudish sleep is Cupid's wronger!

Semplicina
Who has called me?

Archifanfaro
Love! through my love.

Semplicina
Should this dream depart, I would die, love.

Archifanfaro
Not a dream and never to go!

Semplicina
Idol of my dreams, my hopes, my fancies!

Archifanfaro
Live them in factual circumstances.

Semplicina
Life's a dream, then.

Archifanfaro
Day has broken!

Semplicina
Shame has hushed me.

Archifanfaro
Cupid has spoken!

Semplicina & Archifanfaro
Love provides no explanation,
Provides no explanation,
Naught will do save resignation
To his thrall of the bounding heart:
Naught will do save resignation
To his thrall of the bounding heart:
Love demands our resignation
To his thrall-thralldom of the (bounding) heart,
His thralldom of the heart,
(His thralldom of the heart)
For the heart is love's,
For the heart is love's:
Resignation to his thralldom,
In love's demand,
He provides no explanation to loving hearts
For holding the heart,
For holding the heart:
Then accept his shameless traces,
Accept his shameless traces:
Each imprisoned in embraces,
Even could we, would not depart:
Each imprisoned in embraces
Even could we, would not leave them,
Never would we ever part;
(Each imprisoned in embraces, ever)
Give(s) the heart to love:
We're enraptured
To be captured
By love at heart,
We're enchanted
To be granted
A captive heart,

Oh thralldom of the heart!
Oh bounded, bounding heart!
Oh happy start
Of love, my heart!

Curtain

M-4002 • PERMA BOOKS • 35¢
THE GREAT BEST SELLER OF 1954
THE HIGH
TOPAC
AND THE
MIGHTY
Crisis in the air—a novel of men and women face to face with DEATH!
THE COMPLETE BOOK
ERNEST K. GANN

ACT II, SCENE II
Another Room
in the Palace

Archifanfaro has tossed his new subjects, Semplicina excepted, into prison. He will release them only if they promise to abandon their several lunacies. When they unanimously reject this offer, he releases Garbata because she is merry and somewhat less mad than the others. She thereupon joins Semplicina in a plea for the release of their companions. When Archifanfaro grants their suit, all join in prolonged cheers for their King.

Gloriosa, Garbata, Sordidone and Furibondo are discovered in cages, guarded by retainers

Captives   {quartet}
Ever more bitter
Shall be my raging
Cursing the author
Of my encaging;

Unbounded hatred
Lash at my foe,
Well-founded hatred
Lash at my foe,
Disdainful hatred
Lash at my foe
And painful hatred
More baneful grow.
Ever more bitter
Bitterly grow,
Ever more rageful
In my cage grow.
But we are foolish
They are too ghoulish;
Not golden-rulish,
They laugh at woe:
Yes we rage vainly
Since you ungainly
Madmen insanely
Laugh at out woe:
Pity plainly
You do not show,
Pity plainly
You cannot know.

Enter Arcifanfaro and Semplicina

Archifanfaro
What now?
What new forms of madness? Just how
Are these rabid cries meant?
At once be silent or suffer further chastisement!

Gloriosa
My lord, this matchless beauty must roam its own
Queen's Highway.

Sordidone
Set me free to go *my* way.

Malgoverno
If you set me free, sir, I promise I shall pay
Two thousand Ducats when they fall my way.

Furibondo
One moment more as chattel
And I'll smash these bars and roar out to give
        battle.

Gloriosa
I find such confines fearful:
But sweetly make me free and I'll make you
        cheerful.

Archifanfaro
Your plaintive petitions, unreasoned subjects,
        we've attended:
Hear you now how your confinements could soon
        be ended;
You that keep your beauty so vainly, step outside
By surrendering your Pride;
For his freedom the miser
Turn his money's dispassionate despiser;
You will be freed, Your Royal Wildness,
By learning subject mildness;
And the spendthrift earns his exit

When he feels in money the desire to spend and
      checks it.
Knowing how your woes may be righted,
When shall we know you all to your wits united,
Tell me, and your bondage sever?

Gloriosa
Never.

Sordidone
Never.

Sordidone
Never.

Malgoverno
Never.

Furibondo
Never.

Garbata
What will happen to me?
If to gain my freedom I must seem willing to be
Despair's companion, I say, before such
      endeavor:
Never never never never never never never.

Archifanfaro
Your aversion to madness
Is a monstrous merry madness.
We would not keep such a glee dumb.
You have regained your freedom:

86

DUM-dum-dee-DEE-dum!

Garbata is set free

Garbata
Long live King Archifanfaro,
The gods protect his reign!

Semplicina
Long live King Archifanfaro,
That he my lord remain.

Archifanfaro
Such taste excites our favor:
The gods protect our reign!
To Semplicina:
It adds a special flavor
That we your lord remain.

Garbata, Semplicina & Archifanfaro
Long live (We are) Archifanfaro,
The gods protect his (our) reign.
Long live (We are) King Archifanfaro
That he (we) our (my) (your) lord remain.

Garbata
Superb lovely lady,
These bars shall continue
Imposing their shady
Designs on your face.

Gloriosa
Be kind! Show heart! Have grace!

Semplicina
Then, miser, as a lover
Of gold along continue,
But here where now you suffer
Be your biding place.

Sordidone
Be kind! Have heart! Show grace!

Archifanfaro
Let spendthrift passions win you:
To Furibondo:
Your furies continue:
You'll never erase
This doom, this disgrace.

Furibondo & Malgoverno
Oh pity, pity, pity me
To show your grace.

Semplicina & Garbata
We join in their petition,
Their piteous repetition:
Have pity, pity, show your grace!

Archifanfaro *Aside*
Denying all my grace
Would mark my heart as base

Gloriosa, Sordidone, Malgoverno & Furibondo

Oh pity, pity me,
Oh pity, pity me,
Oh pity, pity me!

Semplicina, Garbata & Archifanfaro
Your eyes like beastly curs see,
As though transformed by Circe,
But human mercy
Sets you free!

At a sign from Archifanfaro, the others are released

Tutti
Long live King Archifanfaro
Our city's lord is he:
Long live King Archifanfaro
For gracious clemency.

Semplicina & Garbata
Bow down and kiss his hand who
With mercy can command you,
And show, as you can do,
Humility.

Tutti
Long live King Archifanfaro,
Our city's lord is he:
Long live King Archifanfaro
In gracious clemency:
And long live in our city
Our madness and ga-*ity*
Allowed by the pity
Of majesty!

Maintain our humors witty
And youthful our ditty
Eternally!
Long live King Archifanfaro,
Our city's lord is he:
Long live King Archifanfaro,
Hurrah and fiddle-dee!

Curtain

70-year-old ...
...te in a by-election,
...ed that they were the on...
...ave suffered in world histo...
...members of the Jewish organ...
...tion B'nai B'rith Canada were "ex...
...enists" and "anti-Quebec" an...
...t Jewish neighborhoods in Mont...
...l routinely voted against separat...
...e. He also referred to Jews...
...grants, even though Jews h...
...n Quebec since the late...
...y.
...tion, Mr. Bouchard
...gislature unar...
...ichard's

Arcifanfaro

roi des fous
de laine pure

The Persecution and Assassination of **Jean-Paul Marat**
As Performed by the Inmates of the Asylum of Charenton
Under the Direction of **The Marquis de Sade**

A *Play by* **Peter Weiss**

ACT III, SCENE I
The Royal Garden

Sordidone has buried his coffer of gold under a tree. Malgoverno, who has watched the burial, digs it up and again offers it to Gloriosa, who now accepts it. But Furibondo scares her; she drops the treasure and flees. Thereupon, Furibondo presents it to Garbata, in whose hands the King discovers it. He takes it from her and offers it to Semplicina, who disdains it, whereupon it is returned to Sordidone, who, having come to the conclusion that he can keep it only by melting it down and drinking it, wanders off in search of a crucible.

Sordidone *Discovered burying his coffer*
Earth, our dearest
Good and nearest,
Keep this hidden;
Ancient mother
Let no other
Come unbidden
On this gold:

Darkly, closely,
Wisely, safely,
You that bore him,
Hide and hold.

To your tender
Care I render
All that I love,
Earth eternal,
With maternal
Lullaby love
To enfold:
Darkly, closely,
Wisely, safely,
You that bore him,
Hide and hold.

Deeper, ever deeper,
From the spendthrift wildly
Overbold,
Mother, mildly
Hide and hold.

*Malgoverno appears briefly and, unseen by him,
observes Sordidone*

All my life has been buried!
I have leave to live now unworried,
Unmarried,
Loaf unhurried,
Laugh unharried
And love unflurried!

But at nightfall
Let my sight fall
On my sleeping
Child and bless him,
Then recess him
In your keeping
Far from cold:
Darkly, closely,
Wisely, safely,
You that bore him,
Hide and hold.

How the daring
Thief uncaring
Plays the traitor,
Robs your glory,
Be a story,
Precious mater,
Never told:
Darkly, closely,
Wisely, safely,
You that bore him,
Hide and hold.

Deeper, ever deeper,
From the spendthrift wildly
Overbold,
Mother, mildly
Hide and hold.

*Sordidone exits. Malgoverno re-enters and unburies
the coffer*

Malgoverno
What has the fool committed --
Buried thriving gold alive?
That's too dim-witted!
I'll give sun and fresh air to
What I fall heir to.

Enter Gloriosa

Gloriosa
There's the oaf my beauty could not keep fervent.

Malgoverno
My lady, I'm your servant.

Gloriosa
What's that in your hand, sir?

Malgoverno
To this, *No* was your answer --
It still could serve your beauties;
But I fear you'll meet my offer with a new tease.

Gloriosa
I'll take it as a sequel
When you swear my beauty has no equal.

Malgoverno
On my knees
I swear your beauty outshines Phryne's.

Gloriosa
You are no longer demented.

Malgoverno *Giving her the coffer*
And you shall have this treasure. I am contented.

Gloriosa
As of beauty, she will answer.
Fair exchange and grace advance her
    Charms completely:
    Taking sweetly
    Must enhance her;
Freely giving, then her vow:
I'll be free to be beguiling,
You'll be free to watch me smiling,
And your bondage, I'll allow.

    Here's a smile now
That must do you for a while now.
After all you have my vow
That your bondage I allow.

Furibondo *Enters in a rage*
Stop and drop it! Hop! Hop! hop!

Gloriosa *Dropping the coffer*
Oh my! When fear imposes,
I'm afraid my complexion will lose its roses!

Gloriosa and Malgoverno flee. Furibondo takes the
    coffer

Furibondo
All of this planet,
I cry to each man it

Harbors, rightly in mine!
From high in heaven
The stars combine --
My life was given
The Lion Sign,
On kings, I'll dine --
I am a roaring lion!
How the enthroned ones
Dreadfully pine,
Whimper and whine:
All that they owned once,
This planet, they now must resign,
I'm leonine:
You might with all, oh!
Advance in line!
I'll fight you all, though,
Although you're mine!

I am divine
And so's my Sign:
The world is mine!

Deer in the deer-park
If I should appear, dark
Fearsome slaughters fore-know:
For I shall leap high
On buck and roe,
And quite a heap lie
In tatters low
Before I go --
I am a roaring lion!
Rightly shall might be
Lord of his foe:

Dare they say *No?*
Should the fleas bite me
I'll rub and scratch at them so
They'll whisper *Woe!*
The whole world's my den,
I am Le-O
You'll hear and die, men,
My ho-ho-ho!

Garbata enters

Garbata
And what's unleashed these dreadful roars?

Furibondo
I do as *I* wish. *Giving her the coffer*
Take it all. It's yours.

Furibondo exits

Garbata
It's plainer now and plainer:
A man born insane, ever grows insaner.
And here's the gold. But gold can't laugh and just
        ignores me.
I've already once returned it; and now it bores me.

*Garbata begins to leave. Archifanfaro enters from
        the other side*

Archifanfaro
Come back, that isn't your gold! Do you want
        everything?

Give it at once to your King.

Garbata *Giving him the coffer*
Then take it, I don't want it:
I want a man I've a mind to be kind to!
    My fancy once demanded
    Its joy in gay receiving;
    If love was open-handed,
    I gave my heart away.
    Such fancies have departed;
    The joys of ever giving
    A love that's open-hearted
    I find more truly gay.

So I to harvest go
    And may
No peach or plum deny:
    And say
If you should ask me why,
That never saying no
I find more madly gay.
With any man I'm willing
About the woods to wander
And hear from far and yonder
When horns go tan-ta-ra;
Or sit by crystal fountains
That flow from lofty mountains
And make fond fa-la-la-la-la
And fondly make fa-la-la-la
And fondly fondly make fa-la
We'll fondly fondly make fa-la
We'll fondly make fa-la
We'll make fond fa-la-la.

Garbata exits

Archifanfaro
What a mischief and a load this purse is!
Treasure, they've all forgotten,
When ill-gotten as this hoard,
Under a curse is.
But I, who am their Lord,
If the disposal were mine, I would gladly offer
To Semplicina all the gold in this coffer.
Look at her! She approaches
Without jewels or brooches.

Semplicina enters

Fair damsel! How well met you are!
You be the bigger maiden
And I'll be King Cophetua.
    Goddess, bright as morning,
    Our blessed earth adorning,
    O precious flesh and bone --
    Take my heart, thou fair one,
    Take my heart, thou rare one,
    O take it for thine own --
    Take my heart, thou fair one,
        And share my throne.

    Pity my helpless anguish,
    See how for love I languish,
    Hear how I sigh and groan --
    Pity your lover's moan.
    Waking, dear, and sleeping,

Thou hast my heart in keeping,
I love but thee alone --
Take my heart, thou fair one,
Take my heart, thou rare one,
And share my throne,
And share my throne.

Bowing, he gives her the coffer and exits

Semplicina
Mother always used to tell me
If a gentleman means well, he gives you presents:
When he who gives is a king,
You may expect next day a wedding ring.
But I don't want any treasure,
I've no longing to clutch it,
No desire to touch it
For it gives me no pleasure.
And one who keeps his hold on
All silver things and golden,
I call a miser!

Sordidone *Entering*
A miser or not a miser,
Your head is none the wiser.
Yes, I'm a miser...and fussy,
And that's mine and I want it.

Snatches the coffer from her

You're a hussy!

What a lot I need

What I need
Lots of!
My pot of
Gold's back:
Need I
Hold back?
Indeed I
Must heed it:
I need it!

What good's ev'ry care?
Ev'ry where
Thieves have spied
The heart I must hide.

O where
Is dark or deep enough
That I'd dare
Keep my love
There?

Now I know where,
I know what to do --
First I'll melt it,
Then I'll drink the brew!
Melt well, treasure,
Go where I'd have you!

Sordidone exits

Semplicina
May he not come to harm with his odd potation.
For his thirst is my salvation:

Riches can lead a maiden to ruination.
There's a devil in a ducat
As my grannie used to say,
He lies hid in a ducat
As my grannie used to say,
And an honest maiden may
For the want of gold and silver
On occasion go astray,
By the devil in a ducat lead astray.

A maid who'd travel far,
Said my aged grandmama,
Doesn't mope and grumble
If at times she takes a tumble,
She must take a tumble,
For that is how things are:
If you mean to travel far,
You must tumble and not grumble,
Learn to take things as they are,
Said my aged grandmama.

I will neither mope nor grumble,
I will learn to take a tumble,
I will take things as they are
Like my aged and successful grandmama.

Curtain

ACT III, SCENE II
The Throne Room

Arcifanfaro's subjects demand that he marry. He will choose Gloriosa, Garbata, or Semplicina to be his bride. When Gloriosa and Garbata masquerade as Petrarch's Laura and Helen of Troy, respectively, he discards them both and chooses Semplicina -- who, once crowned queen, instantly turns into a shrieking virago. Arcifanfaro has good reason then when he laments that he is the most foolish of fools.

Arcifanfaro on the throne. The others enter in precession.

Arcifanfaro
Gather, O subjects, about us
And help us find some way to break this deadlock:
We must be joined in wedlock
Quickly before your lunacies unruly
Have magnified our own madness unduly.
Today we have among us three crazy ladies:

Each thinks a crown would suit her,
Gold or pewter.
Let them approach, all three,
So that we may select our bride-to-be.

Gloriosa *approaching*
I'm awed, Lord:
The stars applaud you,
The earth has long adored you,
The very departed, love accord you,
On board the Stygian ferry
Stretch reverent fingers towards you.

Arcifanfaro
Lady, I see that Petrarch never bored you.

Garbata *approaching*
God keep you from the colic,
And costiveness chronic
And spells demonic
And plague demonic
And ills diabolic.

Arcifanfaro
Are you the special tonic
To make me frolic?

Semplicina *approaching*
I'm meek, sir,
Dare not speak, sir,
I feel my limbs grow meek, sir,
Far paler is my cheek, sir,
Than any leek, sir,

For dread lest you should raise your head and
    peek, sir.

Arcifanfaro
Sister thou art to Eros, the fair Greek Sir!
My love!
May I inspire you, fire you, hire you, acquire you
    and attire you!
I desire you, I admire you!

Gloriosa *aside*
Beauty like mine is slated,
As I have often stated,
With a king to be mated
And be feted.

Archifanfaro *aside*
My poor throne would feel sorely over-weighted.

Garbata *aside*
Without qualification
I long for royal station,
Would know the rare sensation
Of coronation.

Archifanfaro *aside*
For such a festival I should need sedation.

Semplicina
To bide me or to hide me?
My heart and my fears divide me:
I blush, I burn: O how shall I decide me?

Archifanfaro
I know you. I'll show you. For you my bride shall
    be!

Gloriosa
You lout, you!
But I flout you!
There's not a thing kingly or noble about you!

Archifanfaro
My poor kingdom must manage to do without you.

Garbata
How mad and bad to choose her
Instead of an amuser:
But I don't care, I say, small fig for you, sir!

Archifanfaro
The fates have rescued me from a Medusa!

Semplicina
My thoughts are buzzing like bees;
My heart is ill at ease.

Archifanfaro
Embrace me!

Semplicina
I shall sneeze.

Archifanfaro
Behold your lover kneeling on his knees!

Semplicina
O please release me! O please!

Archifanfaro
Take my kingdom, take my keys!

Semplicina
What I hear, if you mean it, does not displease:
I'll be Queen of Madmen instead of geese.

Archifanfaro
My beloved!

Semplicina
But not...unless Your Highness agrees
To all His Consort's desires and decrees.

Archifanfaro
What would your wants be, sweetheart?

Semplicina
Well, such as these:
    If you marry me, oh!
    You'll have to be so
    Polite to me: Lo!
    I'll lead you in tow
    Wherever I go,
    I'll lead you in tow:
    If I take a beau
    You're not to say No,
    You're not to say No
    If I take a beau
    You're not to say No.

Archifanfaro
No thank you! Ho-ho!
How quickly I know
My antlers would grow!

Semplicina
If I married you, would
I do as I should,
Be good?
I don't think I could.

Archifanfaro
My bachelorhood!
I'm no babe in the wood:
Be that understood --
No babe in the wood.

Semplicina
If ever I'm led
To the altar and wed,
Though modestly bred
I'll queen it instead,
I'll queen it instead:
Though modestly bred
I'll not be gainsaid
At board or in bed,
At board or in bed
I'll not be gainsaid,
I'll not be gainsaid
At board or in bed!

Archifanfaro
All husbands, I've read,

Wear horns on their head:
I'd sooner be dead!

Semplicina
I might marry you, still
For good or for ill
Or nil
I don't think I will.

Archifanfaro
For Jack to wed Jill
Is pleasant until
Poor Jack gets the bill
And Jack has his fill.

Semplicina
If ever I'm led
To the altar and wed,
I'll not be gainsaid....

Archifanfaro
(No! No!)

Semplicina
At board or in bed.

Archifanfaro
(I'd sooner be dead!)

Semplicina
I'll lead you in tow
Wherever I go,
If I take a beau....

Archifanfaro
(No! No!)

Semplicina
You're not to say no.

Archifanfaro
No no no no no!

Curtain

ACT III, SCENE III
Outside
the City Walls,
as in Act One

The King's subjects now demand to be told the name of their city. He gives each of them a letter of the alphabet. When it develops that one letter is missing, he takes it up himself and moves to the proper position among them so that the onlookers can read the city's name. Then all seven of the protagonists join in the final chorus.

The city gates. All gathered

Chorus
With curiosity all aflame
We've come to know the city's name:
    So say right away!
We ought to know the city's name:
    It's an affront, sir,

If you won't say,
We'll exeunt, sir,
If you won't say,
And stop the play.
A king you may be,
But all the same
You've got to tell us
The city's name.

Arcifanfaro
Quiet, please I implore you! On my ear-drums have
     pity!
What do we call our city?
I wonder. Let us ask our lunatics:
Hither, my dear newcomers, all the six,
All of you draw near me
And hear me:
Very easy the game is:
We're going to find out whether
The six of you and I, your king, together
Are able to discover, say what the name is.
Hola! My grammarians,
My librarians,
Bring the alphabet and give each one a letter,
For Chance may utter the name if we abet Her;
The truth may promptly impose itself,
Without equivocation disclose itself;
And all of you will see
The name that you've already guessed it would be.

Furibondo, Gloriosa, Sordidone, Malgoverno &
Garbata are given letters. They line up and show:
KEW ORN

114

No. The name is not in sight yet.

To Furibondo and Garbata

If you two moved, it might yet.

Furibondo & Garbata change places. The letters read: NEW ORK

No, no, it isn't right yet.
Ah! There's a letter missing in the middle!

Archifanfaro takes a letter and stands in the middle, spelling out NEW YORK

That's what the name is!
That's what the name is!
Answered is your petitions,
Solved is the riddle.
And now my court musicians
Your trumpets, hautboys, tympani,
Your horns and your violins with our voices
        together blending,
Make a joyous ending.

Tutti
The wise and the mad have got
        One world for their dwelling:
But which is which or what
        Is or is not,
        Can baffle telling --
Since naught identifies

Madmen and wise:
Yet they are wisemen who
Have owned their folly.
And all who claim
They're wise we name
Cuckoo!
So you are wise if you
Are madly jolly,
And otherwise
You're cuckoo cuckoo too!

Curtain

Robert Browning's
<u>GOLDONI</u>

Goldoni -- good, gay, sunniest of souls, --
      Glassing half Venice in that verse of thine,
      What though it just reflects the shade and
            shine
Of common life, nor render as it rolls

Grandeur and gloom? Sufficient for thy scrolls
      Was Carnival: Parini's depths enshrine
      Secrets unsuited to that opaline
Surface of things which laughs along thy shoals.

There throng the People: how they come and go,
      Lisp the soft language, flaunt the bright
           garb, -- see, --

On Piazza, Calle, under Portico,
      And over Bridge! Dear King of Comedy,

Be honoured! Thou who didst love Venice so, --
Venice, and we who love her, all love thee!

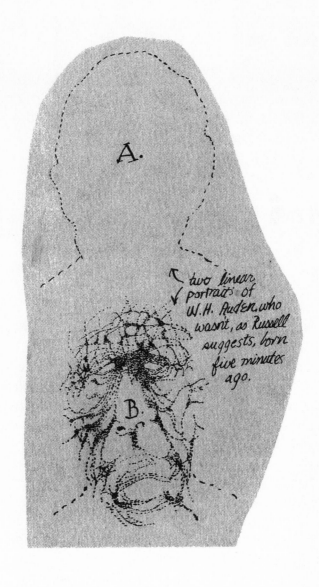

Cover drawing *Unmuzzled OX 3*, 1972 by Laurie Anderson

Selections from our Backlist

Unmuzzled OX 1 (1971) Interview with Robert Creeley. Cover and illustrations by R.Crumb. Poetry by Charles Bukowski, Clark Coolidge, Diane Wakoski, Hugh Seidman, Gary Snyder (staple bound; 68 pages) $25.00

Unmuzzled OX 2 (1972) Interview with James Wright. Cover and illustrations by Crumb. Poetry by Bukowski, Wakosi, Seidman, Robert Bly, Irving Layton; texts by Richard Kostelanetz, W.S. Burroughs, Allen Ginsberg (staple bound; 88 pages) $25.00

Unmuzzled OX 3 **(1972) Interview with W.H. Auden. Cover and art by Laurie Anderson. Epistolary interview/essay with Denise Levertov. Poetry by John Montague, Ed Sanders, Michael Brownstein, John Giorno, Ron Padgett (staple bound; 58 pages)** *SPECIAL TO READERS OF ARCIFANFARO* -- *$7.50*

Unmuzzled OX 4 (1972) Poetry by Ginsberg, Bukowski, Layton, Al Purdy, Margaret Atwood, Daniel Berrigan, Adrienne Rich, Barbara Guest, Michael McClure, David Ignatow (staple bound; 80 pages) $25.00
--edition of 100 signed by Allen Ginsberg, John Wesley and Daniel Berrigan $40.00

Gregory Corso *Writings from OX* (Updating *Unmuzzled OX 5/6* as *Unmuzzled OX 22)* Includes poetry, drawings and interview with Corso, photos by Ginsberg. Fiction by Chandler Brossard, poetry by Edson, Snyder, Marge Piercy, Isabella Gardner. Rochelle Owens on Bukowski (perfect bound;160 pages) $15.00
--signed, cloth edition of 105 $80.00

Gregory Corso *Japanese Notebook OX* World's Longest Poem: ten feet. Accordion folded into a box. Also known as *Earth Egg* $50.00

Unmuzzled OX 7 (1974) Essay on John Wesley by Hannah Green. Art by Ray Johnson. Photos by Gerard Malanga. Poetry by Corso, Atwood, Kenneth Koch, Tony Towle, Anne Waldman, Diane di Prima. First poetry magazine with centerfold: Blondie (staple bound, 80 pages) $20.00

Umuzzled OX 10 (1975) Interviews with Allen Ginsberg and James Dickey. Art by Johnson, Eleanor Antin, Andy Warhol. Poetry by Creeley, Corso, Berrigan, Sanders, McClure, Charles Plymell, Charles Olson, Janine Pomy-Vega, Kenneth Rexroth. Rosalyn Drexler on Rochelle Owens (perfect bound, 128 pages) $30.00

Andrew Wylie *Yellow Flowers* (perfect bound; 36 pages) $7.50

Kenward Elsmlie *Tropicalism* (perfect bound; 80 pages) $20.00

Unmuzzled OX 13 (1976) Fiction by Creeley, Sanders, Kathy Acker. Art by Johnson, Sol LeWitt, John Baldessari, Romare Bearden, William Wiley, General Idea. Comics by James Schuyler and Joe Brainard. Journals by Carolee Schneemann, Hannah Weiner. Poetry by Ginsberg, Bill Knott, Andrei Codrescu, Lou Reed   (perfect bound; 160 pages) $25.00

Unmuzzled OX 14 (1976) Cover and art by Hannah Wilke. Interviews with Warhol, Robert Indiana, Eugene McCarthy, Robert Duncan. Poetry by Olson, Bukowski, William Staffford. Lawrence Alloway on Malcom Morley. Claes Oldenburg. Comics by Brainard & Padgett (perfect bound; 130 pages) $25.00

Unmuzzled OX 15 (1977) Djuna Barnes interviews with Zeigfeld, Kiki, James Joyce; other interviews with Phil Glass, Kate Millet, Gary Snyder, Pierre Trudeau. Art by Wilke, Paul Thek, Pat Steir. Poetry by McClure, Ted Berrigan, John Ashbery (perfect bound; 140 pages) $25.00

Poets' Encyclopedia (1979) The World's Basic Knowledge Traversed and Transformed by 225 Poets, Artists, Musicians and Novelists (320 pages) Perfect bound: $30.00. Cloth: $50.00. Signed by 100 contributors: $100.00

The Cantos (121-125) Ezra Pound (1984) Extensions of Pound's cantos, satiric and otherwise, by Ginsberg, A.M. Klein, Jackson MacLow. Writing through Ezra Pound (and A.M. Klein) by Cage (tabloid; pages 1-24 with extra matter) $7.50

The Cantos (125-143) Ezra Pound (1986) Photos by Malanga, Diane Arbus. Art by Lewitt, Komar & Melamid. Extensions by Ginsberg, Creeley, Corso, Giorno, McCarthy, Henry Korn, R. Buckminster Fuller, James Lee Byers & John Brockman (tabloid; pages 24-64 with extra matter) $7.50

Canto (144) Ezra Pound : Blues 10 (1988) Edited by Charles Henri Ford. **Virgil Thomson on Words and Emotions in Music** (tabloid; pages 40-90 with extra matter) **Special with larger order: $2.00**

The Cantos (145-150) Ezra Pound's Interview (1987) First publication of Ezra Pound's Cantos 78-79 in English. Interview with Daniel Berrigan (tabloid; pages 85-120 with extra matter) $7.50

The Cantos (121-150) Ezra Pound (1992) Collecting the four tabloids. Cloth $100.00

Unmuzzled OX XIV (1996) **Poems to the Tune by Johnson, Creeley, Elmslie.** Poets' Guide to Canada by Berrigan, Atwood, Edson, Warren Woessner (perfect bound; 100 pages) $9.95

Prices quoted are U.S. funds. Canadian orders add 30%. We pay postage. **Unmuzzled OX** 105 Hudson Street New York 10013

Man Reading an *Unmuzzled OX* by Colette

Ray Johnson, others

The Death of Marat, after David, the cover and frontispiece by **Colette,** document a performance at PS 1 in 1977. In 1985, Colette designed costumes for the Berlin Opera's production of *L'Heure Espagnole*; on page 16 she portrays Ravel's Auspenta, and this Auspenta could be Dittersdorf's Semplicina. Or not. On page 50, *Last Call for Romance* (1983-84) is a painted photograph; page 63 is *Olympia* (1992); and on page 92, *Justine Goes to Hollywood* is a a large 4ft by 6ft color photo (edition 3) (1981). The Kim Foster Gallery recently held a retrospective of Collette's work..

Sharon Gilbert's collages -- opposite, on the back cover, and on page 46 -- were done particularly for this first edition of *Arcifanfaro*. Sharon Gilbert's work has recently been shown at the Brooklyn Museum.

Giambattista Tiepolo was a Venetian friend of Goldoni. His work has elegantly illustrated other editions of Goldoni's plays.

COLETTE   JESSICA   COLETTE   JESSICA